30 DAYS TO
STOP NAIL BITING:
A JOURNAL FOR ADULTS

This journal belongs to

_____

Hi there and welcome to your journal!

I wanted to create this journal to help people like me, adults who have struggled to stop biting their nails. I have tried everything there is and wanted to share how I managed to stop biting my nails at the age of 34, after biting them for close to 27 years from the age of 7.

Before you begin, I want you to promise that you will be open to trying everything mentioned in this journal. Remember that you are here to try something new, so why not just go with the flow?! Also remind yourself that, by starting on this journal, you have already taken the first step to stop biting your nails, so well done!

I have also included extra pages so that you can keep journaling after your 30 days or, if needed, can give it another go if you slip (which can happen to the best of us!). Remember that this is not a medical approach and therefore makes no guarantees about your success, rather it will keep you on track and guide you along the way; using it will help you to stop biting your nails – it did for me!

Without further ado, let's get started on your journey to stop biting your nails. Get yourself a good pen and let's begin on the next page! Remember to write freely without stopping to think too much. Just leave it all on the page and look back later.

Enjoy and stay on the path – you can do it!
Stephen Beale

DAY 1: Why do you want to do this? What would it mean to you to stop biting your nails?

DAY 2: Picture your nails after not biting them for 30 days. When you look at your hands, what will you see? What will those you care about see?

DAY 3: Describe your earliest memories of biting your nails. How did you feel at that time? Was there anything in your life that was happening at the time?

DAY 4: Think about times in the past when you've tried to stop. How far did you get? What brought you back to nail biting?

DAY 5: What have you tried to help you stop biting your nails in the past? What was your reason for trying each of these things? Were other people involved?

DAY 6: Think about times when you feel the urge to bite your nails. What goes through your mind? Try to slow it down and describe the whole process in detail.

DAY 7: On balance, what are the pros and cons of biting your nails? Go into as much detail as you can here.

"Whether you think you can, or you think you can't, you're right."

Henry Ford

Founder of Ford Motor Company

DAY 8: What signs or symptoms do you notice when you are about to bite your nails? Think about your movements, thoughts and/or behaviour.

DAY 9: Are there any specific situations which may trigger you to want to bite your nails? Think about what happens around you and how that makes you feel.

DAY 10: Look back at day 9. What sort of things could you say in your head to slow down the process or prevent you from biting your nails again?

DAY 11: Think about all the other behaviours that come along with your nail biting. Try to put them in order, from first to last and what causes each one.

DAY 12: If you feel the urge to bite your nails again, what things can you do to stop you from slipping back into the habit?

DAY 13: If you do slip a little and bite a nail here and there, what positive things can you tell yourself to get back on track?

DAY 14: What treatments or tricks have you tried that have been most helpful so far? Why do you think they worked for you?

"Few things in the world are more powerful than a positive push. A smile. A world of optimism and hope. A 'you can do it' when things are tough."

Richard M. Devos

Businessman

DAY 15: Write freely about how it has made you feel to get this far without biting your nails. Let it flow!

DAY 16: Think about your social calendar over the next few months or year. Are there any times in it when you think you will most likely slip back into nail biting? Why?

DAY 17: Look back at yesterday's notes. What things can you put in place or do to make sure you don't slip? Be as specific as you can.

DAY 18: Now think about your sleep. How well have you been sleeping lately? Has this impacted on your nails in any way?

DAY 19: Thinking more about sleep, when do you feel you get the best sleep? What helps you to achieve this? Is there anything which stops you sleeping well?

DAY 20: How about your work-life balance – is this in order? Does it ever feel imbalanced? Why? If not, how can you maintain that harmony?

DAY 21: Well done! 3 weeks in. Look back over the last 3 weeks (in your head, or your notes here). What have been some of the highs? Are you having any problems still?

"Once you believe in yourself and you put your mind to something, you can do it."

Simone Biles

Gymnast, Olympic Gold Medalist

DAY 22: Imagine you feel a sudden, irrational urge to bite your nails. What thoughts or phrases can you tell yourself to slow things down and avoid the dreaded bite?

DAY 23: Imagine you have got this far and slip back into biting your nails. Write some words to yourself describing how you feel and the situation that might have caused it.

DAY 24: Now visualise someone you care about seeing you biting your nails. What might they say to you to help you to stop?

DAY 25: Think ahead to a big moment in your life that is coming up where you might feel a little anxious. What plans will you put in place to avoid the dreaded slip back to biting?

DAY 26: How do you feel having got this far on your journey to no more nail biting? What would mean to you stop biting your nails forever?

DAY 27: What activities or things do you do that make you forget just about everything else? How often have you been doing them lately? What impact has this had on your life?

DAY 28: Think about all the places in your life. Describe the main 3-4 places below and how you feel in each environment.

"Don't watch the clock. Do what it does: keep going"

Sam Levenson

Comedian and Presenter

DAY 29: What accessories, tools or gadgets can you take with you everywhere which can help you to avoid biting or picking?

DAY 30: You made it! Think back about the last 30 days. Describe your thoughts and feelings, and also look forward to your next 30 days – what happens next on your journey?

You did it!

Well done!

There's plenty more space in this journal to keep the inspiration going – just turn over and get creative!

Journal Entry - Date: _____ / _____ / _____

Journal Entry - Date: _____ / _____ / _____

Journal Entry - Date: _____ / _____ / _____

Journal Entry - Date: ___ / ___ / ___

Journal Entry - Date: ____ / ____ / ____

Journal Entry - Date: ...... / ...... / ......

Journal Entry - Date: ___ / ___ / ___

Journal Entry - Date: _____ / _____ / _____

Journal Entry - Date: ...... / ...... / ......

Journal Entry - Date: _____ / _____ / _____

Journal Entry - Date: ___ / ___ / ___

Journal Entry - Date: ____ / ____ / ____

Journal Entry - Date: ____ / ____ / ____

Journal Entry - Date: _____ / _____ / _____

Journal Entry - Date: ___ / ___ / ___

Journal Entry - Date: _____ / _____ / _____

Journal Entry - Date: ____ / ____ / ____

Journal Entry - Date: _____ / _____ / _____

Journal Entry - Date: ___ / ___ / ___

Journal Entry - Date: _____ / _____ / _____

Journal Entry - Date: _____ / _____ / _____

Journal Entry - Date: .... / .... / ....

Journal Entry - Date: _____ / _____ / _____

Journal Entry - Date: _____ / _____ / _____

Journal Entry - Date: ...... / ...... / ......

Journal Entry - Date: ___ / ___ / ___

Journal Entry - Date: _____ / _____ / _____

Journal Entry - Date: ___ / ___ / ___

Journal Entry - Date: .... / .... / ....

Journal Entry - Date: _____ / _____ / _____

Journal Entry - Date: _____ / _____ / _____

Doodle Space

Doodle Space

Doodle Space

Doodle Space

Doodle Space

Doodle Space

Doodle Space

Doodle Space

Shopping List for Nail Biters

1. Nail biting ointment

I'm sure you've tried using this before but, there are few ways in which I'm sure it can help you still. The most helpful for me has been to buy several bottles at one time. I don't keep one at home, one at work, and one in my bag. This means I always have something on hand and can reapply as needed. I know it does not stop you from biting your nails, but the foul taste can be a subtle reminder because it often only comes after the fact. Either way, this helps to remind you of what you are doing. Even when you innocently handle food and this polish/ointment leaves a bitter taste on that food, that can still be a reminder that you don't want to do this anymore.

2. Nail clippers

Go out and buy yourself two pairs of good quality nail clippers. Again, one can be to keep in your bathroom cabinet at home and then others can be to carry in your bag. The reason why I said good quality is that it will likely make you want to use them, and not feel like you've wasted your money buying something you don't use.

Also, be aware that leaving your nails to grow extremely long will not help you to stop biting them. I have relapsed into nail-biting several times after I refused to clip my nails and ended up picking them because they became too long and annoying. Clip them at regular intervals and try to smooth them off so that they don't become Sharp and draw your attention any more than they should.

3. Mindfulness

Try using the free version of the Headspace app to help you bring a bit of mindfulness into dealing with your nail biting. I found this particularly useful and stuck with it for several weeks when I first managed to stop biting my nails. Be consistent and it only needs a few minutes of your day. After a few days, you should start to feel clearer and more aware of the thought process behind your nail biting.

4. Moisturiser / skin cream

This really helped me because, along with nail biting, I would generally pick the skin around my fingers as a first sign that I was going to bite my nails. When this grows back, this can often be very hard and easy to pick. My wife then put me onto using coconut oil to soften the skin around my hands. I found this had a positive effect on picking at skin and I managed to stop doing it shortly thereafter. Remember to apply it frequently and make a habit of it. Doing this should also make you appreciate your skin and nails that much more, especially if you do it daily.

5. Fidget cube

know this might sound silly, but this is another thing that really helped me. I found that after I stop biting my nails, my hands were fidgety and always looking for something to do. I tried to use a fidget spinner but that didn't really work, and it was also quite noisy so it bothered other people in my office. I then noticed the fidget cubes, which are bigger but still weigh next to nothing and, crucially, have some silent parts to them so you can use them at your desk without annoying colleagues. You can get them extremely cheaply on Amazon or eBay so find the one that looks best for you, ideally with at least six different things for your hands to do. Again, try taking this with you in your bag wherever you go so you can pull it out at key points.

6. Hypnotherapy CD/session

've put this in as an optional extra but I know it did help me. I was extremely sceptical about hypnotherapy, so I bought a CD from Amazon. This was several years ago and they weren't many other options, but now you can find many of these on YouTube but the CD I got was good and worked very well. If you're still struggling with nail biting after all the other things in this book, then look into this as one option. The hypnosis side really isn't quite what you might think, it's much more about being relaxed and just thinking about aspects related to nail-biting than it is about an out-of-body experience and doing silly things!

Strategies

1. Early nights

I've read several books on sleeping and the importance of sleep and am now extremely aware that getting to bed early is an incredibly helpful thing to do. Giving yourself enough chance to recover and rest through sleep is not only free, but also one of the easiest changes you can make in your life. If you feel that you don't have enough time to sleep, are there any things that you might be able to cut out to make way for a little bit more time in bed? You might also want to consider having digital and caffeine curfews at least one hour before bed as I know this was extremely helpful for me in terms of getting to sleep, especially on nights before work.

2. Sleep tracking

In line with the points above about early nights, it's also helpful to keep some kind of sleep log or track of your sleep. The best way that I found to do this is through using my Fitbit. This gives me a fairly accurate idea of how many hours I've slept at night and it's automatic so I don't need to think about it. I try not to obsess over the readings, but I also try to remember to give myself enough time to fall asleep and get my 7.5 hours' sleep per night. I say this number because it is the number I have found that I need to function properly – you can find yours by tracking it for a few weeks. I often notice the negative effects on my productivity when I have not giving myself enough time to sleep, perhaps only sleeping around 6 and 1/2 hours. I tend to feel these effects that same day or the day after without fail. Try to see what works for you and stay on top of this because it is the easiest and best way to help yourself feel better and get some added clarity.

3. Open conversations

From my studies in health, I can tell you that the acknowledged first step for just about any psychological aspect of a health problem is to have a conversation about it. Obviously nail biting is a sensitive topic so you will want to choose who to talk about this. But having a conversation can help you to see another perspective on the topic and to look to working towards a solution. Try to have the mindset that nothing is taboo when it comes to your health. If you can think of a friend or family member with whom you feel comfortable discussing this with, then seek them out and ask them for a little bit of their time to chat about it as soon as you can.

4. Addressing sources of concern/anxiety directly

Hopefully your journal notes will have helped you to pinpoint some of the concerns that might be leading you to bite your nails, or anything which is a source of anxiety. With this in mind, try to take some direct steps to address these and put an action plan in place. You may not be able to remove all of them all together, but you can at least be mindful of their impact on you and be prepared for that. But, if possible, do what you can to remove them! Anything which is having a negative effect on you is something to address and look at in more detail as soon as you can. This change might be quite difficult, but it will certainly help you on your path to stop nail biting.

5. Reducing stimulant use

Stimulants can cause imbalances in your body, manifesting in changes in your moods and emotions. No doubt you are aware that your emotions can play a part in biting your nails. So, anything that causes a disturbance in your emotions should be treated with care. Common stimulants include caffeine, tobacco, alcohol and many forms of drugs (legal or pharmaceutical). Look at how you are consuming these and whether you can reduce or remove them from your diet and lifestyle. Small amounts may be OK but be mindful of their impact on your day to day life.

Techniques Log

Technique   **Notes**

Techniques Log

Technique

Notes

Made in the USA
Columbia, SC
23 April 2019